DARTM

Walks with an
All-Terrain Pushchair

By Emma Richardson

FOREST PUBLISHING

First published in 2005 by FOREST PUBLISHING,
Woodstock, Liverton, Newton Abbot, Devon TQ12 6JJ

British Library Cataloguing in Publication Data

A catalogue record for this book is available from the British Library.

ISBN 0 9536852 9 2

Forest Publishing

Editorial by:

Mike Lang

Printed and bound in Great Britain by:

Wotton Printers Limited, Newton Abbot, Devon TQ12 4PJ

Dedication

For my wonderful family.

Contents

Acknowledgement

I should like to express my sincere appreciation to the Dartmoor National Park Authority for advice and assistance given during the preparation of this book.

Introduction

Having purchased an All-Terrain Pushchair (ATP) because of a love of the outdoors and through a desire to expose my children to the joys of walking, I couldn't believe that no walking books existed for this purpose. I then set out to write such a book and determined to make it equally interesting, challenging and encouraging for other young families.

It is important that I mention some points of safety and remind walkers that it is their own responsibility to take suitable safety precautions when out walking. Dartmoor is notoriously unpredictable and your safety should never be taken for granted, particularly when walking with children.

Always carry a compass and know how to use it. Weather conditions can change rapidly, so it is important to be aware of your location at all times.

Carry a map. The most suitable map for this area is the Ordnance Survey Explorer OL 28: Dartmoor. The maps provided for each walk are sketch maps only and are not intended as a sole means of navigation.

Wear suitable clothing and footwear; even in good weather consider carrying a raincoat. I also extend 'being prepared' to taking a supply of drink - water, most importantly - and food. Snacks such as dried fruit and chocolate provide good sources of energy for the tired walker. Walking with babies and toddlers also necessitates taking a nappy, wipes and a nappy bag, although I would use a coat in place of a changing mat to save on space. In summer, sunhats and cream are also a good idea.

Tell someone where you are going, particularly if you are new to

Dartmoor, walking alone or are inexperienced. Do not rely on a mobile phone to get you out of difficulty. They are useful, but you may not always be able to receive a signal on all parts of the moor.

Walk locations and difficulty

Each walk is designed to be suitable for all members of the family and includes several areas of historical interest which will hopefully provide discussion points and a focus for your day out. The routes I have selected vary in length and difficulty, denoted by a star-rating system as below.

*   Very easy terrain, suitable for a solo walker or wheelchair.
**   Mixed terrain, with some harder sections or manoeuvring required; solo walking possible but challenging.
*** Physically demanding; two adults required for lifting the pushchair in some sections.

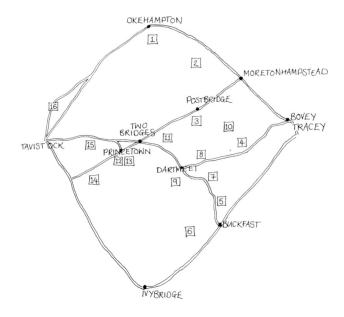

Walk No.	Walk Name	Difficulty
1.	Belstone	**
2.	Scorhill Circle	**
3.	Golden Dagger Mine	**
4.	Haytor and Haytor Quarry	**
5.	Holne Village and Horseshoe Falls	***
6.	Shipley Bridge and Avon Dam	*
7.	Mel Tor and Dr Blackall's Drive	***
8.	Babeny and Sherwell	*
9.	The Swincombe Valley	**
10.	Hound Tor and Greator Rocks	**
11.	Bellever Forest	*
12.	Nun's Cross I	**
13.	Nun's Cross II	*
14.	Burrator and Crazywell Pool	* or **
15.	King's Tor and Two Quarries	**
16.	Brent Tor	**

Suggested techniques

All the walks in this book have been tried and tested with an ATP, and most single-handedly. The following suggestions may help in negotiating tricky areas.

- Take your time, particularly over rough terrain.
- If your ATP has a wrist-strap, use it - particularly on hilly stretches.
- Stile crossings (and there is only one walk which contains them) are a two-person operation. The only safe way to cross a stile with an ATP is to take the child out, pass him or her over the stile to the other adult and then lift the ATP over separately.

Finally, I should like to draw your attention to the Dartmoor National Park Authority's 'Walking with Moor Care and Less Wear Code of Conduct':-

- Travel with Moor Care - try and share transport and if possible use public transport. If you do have to use a car, keep within the 40 mph speed limit on moorland roads and park sensibly using only hardened parking areas in wet weather.
- Walk only where you have a right, are allowed to do so, or are clearly welcome. Come prepared with an up-to-date map.
- Always use gates and stiles to cross boundaries.
- If you are following the line of an eroded path stick to it, and avoid widening it, by walking in single file if necessary. Respect signs asking you to avoid very badly eroded paths.
- Avoid climbing straight up or down steep hills. Take a winding route to avoid damage.
- When the ground is wet, plan your route carefully and use hard surfaces where possible thus avoiding vulnerable, waterlogged moorland paths.
- Take care not to cause disturbance to wildlife or livestock, particularly during the moorland lambing and bird breeding season (1 March to 15 July) and during the lambing season on enclosed farmland (1 December to 30 June).
- Dartmoor is rich in archaeological remains and many sites are protected by law. Learn how to recognise archaeological features and ensure that you don't disturb them; in particular never move stones, dig, light fires, or bivouac in or around archaeological sites.
- Respect local byelaws and footpath/bridleway diversions (as signposted) and follow the Countryside Code.
- Please remember that all of the National Park is owned by someone and respect the interests of those who own the land or make a living from it.
- If you have a dog, follow the advice for dog owners in the Walking Code of Conduct.*
- If you are camping, follow the Camping and Backpacking Code of Conduct.*

  * Further information available from DNP Information Centres.

I hope that you will enjoy these walks as much as my family and I enjoyed researching them. Together I hope we can help to create the next generation of walkers who will enjoy the endless delights of Dartmoor.

Emma Richardson
January 2005

1. Belstone

Start and finish point: SX 621 938.
Distance: 6 km.
Degree of difficulty: ** Moderately challenging, with some rough and uphill terrain.
Brief description: A walk onto the northern moor that begins in the beautiful village of Belstone and includes a visit to a stone circle and part of the East Okement valley.

This walk begins from the car park on Brenamoor Common, at the entrance to Belstone village. Turn left out of the car park and follow the main road through the village.

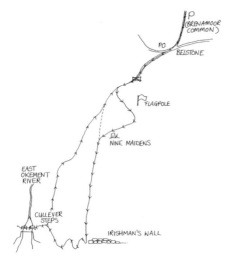

Belstone is an interesting mixture of old traditional cottages and large Victorian buildings, with many remnants of times past still to be seen if one looks carefully. The alert amongst you will notice the village stocks and the small manor pound. When mentioning these in his famous 'Guide to Dartmoor' (first published in 1909), William Crossing also referred to pillars between which formerly swung a ducking stool, so it is clear that at one time Belstone was a village keen on punishment!

On reaching a small village green where the road forks, take the

8

right-hand fork and walk past the unusual-looking post office (formerly a chapel), complete with its red telephone box. Follow the road straight ahead. It climbs increasingly steeply towards the moor. Go through the gate onto the moor and continue to follow the track uphill. A little further on, as you appear to reach the top of the incline, you should notice the summit of Belstone Tor appearing to your left. At this point take the grassy track, also to your left, following it uphill and keeping the flagpole on your left. As you reach the plateau (to the right of the flagpole), stop and take in the view. To your right is the East Okement valley and to the left is the Taw valley, with Cosdon Hill in the distance.

Continue to follow the track heading towards the base of Belstone Tor until you pass a series of small pits on your right. Just beyond the pits turn right and proceed downhill; walk as if heading straight towards East Bowden/Higher Halstock Farm on the far side of the East Okement valley. As you approach another track, you will see the prehistoric stone circle known as the Nine Maidens in front of you.

The Nine Maidens

In spite of its name, the circle actually consists of sixteen stones - not all still standing - but, according to William Crossing, there were seventeen when he wrote his 'Guide to Dartmoor' and it was sometimes known as the Seventeen Brothers. It is generally believed that the circle surrounded a cist (burial feature), and it is said that the stones were once maidens who met here to dance on the Sabbath; for this wicked act they were turned to stone and are now compelled to dance every day at noon.

Continue down the hill to pick up the track. Turn left along it. Follow this track as it contours along the base of Belstone Tor. Sometimes it is rough in places (and particularly after heavy rain) and you may need to deviate to the left or right for short stretches.

The track rises gently and below you, to your right, the enclosures of East Okement Farm should now be visible. Just beyond the northern end of these enclosures the convergence of several tracks may also be seen. This is Cullever Steps and to where you are now heading. Take the track that zig-zags down to this point. Cross over the bridges and enjoy the view back up towards the Belstone Tors, noticing a very straight wall running up and over the hill - this is Irishman's Wall.

The Belstone Tors
and Irishman's Wall from
Cullever Steps (Author)

Several years ago an Irishman set about trying to enclose an area of the moor for his own use. He brought several of his countrymen with him to carry out the work. The local men of Belstone and Okehampton were not happy about this as it would cut them off from areas of the moor that they themselves farmed, so they waited until work had neared completion and then set about ruining large sections of the wall. This was enough to cause the builder to move elsewhere.

Cullever Steps is the name for the river crossing, derived from the fine sets of stepping-stones used for paving the fords on the East Okement River and the Black-a-ven Brook. This crossing has, in fact, evolved with the use of the moor, the fords having been paved for gun carriages and the current girder bridges, of much more recent date, having been provided for modern-day military vehicles. An interesting discovery was made near here in 1935 when a knife of pale grey flint, approximately four and a half inches long, surfaced after rain. Experts decided that it was probably 'Beaker' i.e. early Bronze Age - about 2000BC.

Cross back over the two bridges and take the track to your left (there is a sign at the start of the track: 'No MOD vehicles beyond this point'). Follow this track back up the hill to return to Belstone village.

Part of Belstone village

2. Scorhill Circle

Start and finish point: SX 663 867.
Distance: 2.5 km.
Degree of difficulty: ** Fairly easy terrain apart from a short, very rocky section in the initial stages.
Brief description: This ramble over open moorland includes a number of interesting features and potential picnic spots. During summer months, the walk could be combined with a visit to the superb open-air swimming pool at nearby Chagford.

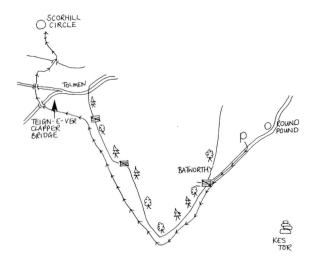

Park just off the road, after passing 'Round Pound'. Leave the car and walk along the road towards Batworthy. Just before the bridge at the entrance to the Batworthy estate, take the rocky path that follows the stream uphill, keeping the walls and trees on your right. The next 250 metres of the walk is very demanding and is best tackled by two adults. Continue to follow the rocky path as it ascends gently and opens out onto rough moorland, at the same time following the line of the wall and picking out the best route you can.

On reaching the end of the wall - Batworthy Corner - look back for a superb view of Kestor Rock. You have now negotiated the hardest section of the walk. Continue around the corner, keeping the wall on your right. You will follow this wall almost to its very end. At times there are short sections of path. On the whole, the terrain is easily negotiable and, providing you use the wall as your 'handrail', keeping it on your right, you will not get lost.

After approximately 500 metres the wall is punctuated by a wooden five-bar gate. Continue past this until, after about a further 250 metres, you reach another. From here the ground starts to fall away abruptly and you should be able to pick out Scorhill Circle, situated directly ahead on the brow of the opposite hill. Closer to hand, below you and leftwards, you will also see two clapper bridges, the nearer of these spanning the North Teign River and re-erected only a few years ago, in 1999, after having fallen victim to a storm in the 19th century.

The reinstated clapper bridge
over the North Teign River

Clapper bridges, so much a feature of Dartmoor, were usually built on medieval pack-horse routes across the moor to enable travellers to cross streams and rivers in safety.

Head straight towards the clapper bridge over the North Teign River - as you descend towards the river, you will pick up a track taking you directly there. This spot is relatively easily accessible and yet normally as secluded as if one were in the middle of the moor. Take some time for a picnic, a rest and, if walking with older children, see if you can find the Teign-e-ver clapper bridge and also the Tolmen - a large rock with a hole in it - lying on the bed of the river close to the opposite bank.

This hole in the rock was made by small pebbles swirled by the water when the river was much higher. Legend has it that this stone has healing powers. Anyone who passes through the hole is said to be cured of rheumatism. I wouldn't recommend trying this for yourself, however!

Cross the reinstated clapper bridge carefully and follow the track straight ahead to Wallabrook Bridge, which was the second clapper bridge you saw earlier. After going over this bridge, follow the track that ascends a rather bumpy headland and leads you to the Gidleigh Leat. (There is an alternative track up the gully to the side of the headland that also leads you to the Gidleigh Leat.) From there, cross the leat by means of the little clapper bridge and then continue to follow the track, heading in a northerly direction, until you arrive at Scorhill Circle.

Scorhill Circle

Scorhill Circle is one of the most impressive stone circles on the moor and, in common with others, has been the subject of much speculation over the years, both as regards its origin and purpose. Almost ninety feet in diameter and dating from the late neolithic/early Bronze Age, it most probably had great ritual significance. Gruesome stories have been told about ancient sacrifice on the site, and some say it is home to a giant, or troll, who feasts on local sheep!

Having looked around the stones at your leisure, take the track that heads back from whence you came. The route back to your car is simply to retrace your steps. On returning to your vehicle, you may be interested to take a short detour to look at Round Pound, which you drove past before setting out on the walk.

Tree on Round Pound
(Author)

These remains have great archaeological significance, forming part of a large settlement here. The site consists of hut circles and field enclosures and is in close proximity to many ceremonial monuments - mostly on Shoveldon. In addition to this, William Crossing writes of a significant find of flint implements being made on the Batworthy estate in 1887. He adds that by 1889 the then owner of the estate, Mr F. N. Budd, had discovered 6,400 specimens, many of which were of a type of stone found at Sidmouth. It was believed that the material had been brought to Batworthy from Sidmouth by the primitive settlers, and the field enclosure where they were found was actually the site of manufacture of these primitive implements - arrowheads, knives, scrapers etc.

3. Golden Dagger Mine

Start and finish point: SX 676 811.

Distance: 3 km.

Degree of difficulty: ** Easy terrain, with one moderate climb on the return route.

Brief description: A delightfully easy ramble through part of the intriguing remnants of Dartmoor's tin mining past. This walk will enable you to visit what is left of the last working tin mine on Dartmoor.

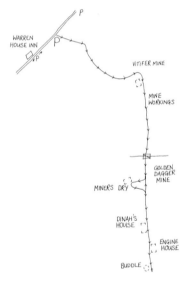

Park in the small car park on the south-eastern side of the road just before reaching the Warren House Inn from the Moretonhampstead direction. Then set off eastwards along the marked track, heading away from the road. Behind you, and to the right, is the famous Warren House Inn.

At approximately 430 metres above sea level it has been claimed that the Warren House Inn is the highest pub in the country, although it is actually the third highest. The building itself dates back to 1845, when it was erected to replace an even earlier pub situated on the other side of the road. It is said that at that time smouldering peat from the fireplace of the older pub was carried across the road by shovel and placed in the new fireplace of the Warren House Inn, and that since then the fire has never gone out. Appropriately, the pub is named after a nearby rabbit warren, rabbits having been introduced onto the moor, possibly in Norman times, to provide a source of food.

Continue to follow the track as it starts to gently descend the hill, pausing now and again to admire the views. If you have not already done so, you should be able to pick out at least one of the four enclosures known as the 'Four Aces', situated to your left on the lower slopes of Birch Tor.

The Warren House Inn

The story of the Four Aces is part of Dartmoor legend and concerns the wicked Jan Reynolds of Widecombe. Apparently he had once entered into a pact with a stranger - who, it seemed, was the Prince of Darkness himself. Jan, however, failed to keep this pact: during the great thunderstorm that damaged Widecombe church on Sunday, 21st October 1638, he was whisked away on the back of the Devil's black horse. Then, as they passed over Birch Tor, Jan dropped some playing cards that he was holding in his hand and these became transformed into the four stone enclosures that can be seen to this day.

Soon the track bends to the left and deposits you amongst the remains of the Vitifer Mine workings. Before long it will also lead you to a beautiful spot with a stream, grassy area and many interesting ruins. This provides an excellent place for a picnic, and

Part of the remains of the
Vitifer Mine workings

those wishing only for a short walk could terminate their ramble here. (Please be aware that there are still many mineshafts and deep pools of water just off the track and all around this area. Please supervise children closely to avoid accidents.)

Once you have explored this area, resume your walk along the track, now heading southwards towards Soussons Plantation. On reaching an old wooden gate, go straight through it, making sure you shut it behind you. A little further on there is a signpost. Turn right here towards some ruined buildings - these are the first of the remains that you will see of the Golden Dagger Mine.

This small ruin was the 'Miners' Dry', a building provided with heat so that miners finishing their work underground had somewhere to change and dry their clothes.

Retrace your steps to the signpost and then continue to follow the track southwards to the next ruin, where an information board provides many interesting facts about the mine workings and remains.

This building is known as Dinah's House and was last occupied in the early 1940s. All the remains seen here date from the 19th century or early 20th century; in fact, the name 'Golden Dagger' was first recorded in the 1850s.

18

Continue along the track to the remains of the engine house - on the left.

The engine house was built in 1920 and contained machinery driven by water, gas and steam.

A little further along the track you will reach the conclusion of your walk - the 'buddle' - and the final remains of Golden Dagger.

The buddle was a circular mechanism involved in the sifting of the tin ore.

Return to your car by retracing your steps. You may want to reward your family with some refreshments at the Warren House Inn, a family-friendly establishment.

Remains of the 'buddle'
(Author)

4. Haytor and Haytor Quarry

Start and finish point: SX 765 771.
Distance: 3 km.
Degree of difficulty: ** An initial steep climb, but otherwise easy terrain.
Brief description: A fascinating tour of the Haytor area, where you will see part of a 19th century granite tramway and the remains of a quarry with parts of the old machinery still in place. Haytor also offers splendid views that, on a clear day, extend as far as the English Channel.

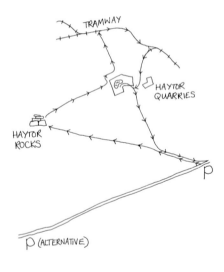

Park in the Haytor lower car park. Here there are toilet facilities and an information centre. In busier periods you may need to park in the car park further up the hill, from where you will easily be able to pick up the walk.

Cross the road and follow the broad green track up to Haytor Rocks. Any of the green tracks can be taken, but some are steeper than others! Take your time as this is quite a long hard push, but worth it for the fantastic views.

The ominous position of Hay Tor makes it seem all the larger. Situated right on the edge of the moor, it can be seen from as far away as the English Channel. If one looks carefully, steps may be seen cut into the tor to assist the climber! These were fashioned in Victorian times and used to be accompanied by an iron handrail.

Haytor Rocks

It is perhaps no surprise that this dramatic tor has been used to dramatic purpose. For example, it 'played' Camelot in the 1953/4 film 'Knights of the Round Table' starring Stanley Baker, Mel Ferrer, Robert Taylor and Ava Gardner.

Looking out from
Haytor Rocks (Author)

Walk around the base of Hay Tor to its easternmost point and then head downhill to pick up a small track: initially this track is hard to make out, but if you walk towards the spoil tips of Haytor Quarry, which are visible lower down the hill, it will become more obvious and lead you to the far, left-hand, corner of the fence around the quarry itself. Turn left here, follow the track around the mound in front of you and continue for the short distance to the spot where it is crossed by a large, straight track that was part of the old granite tramway. At this point turn left again, proceed along the large track for approximately 350 metres until you reach the main part of the tramway and then turn right to follow its course eastwards. You will now notice just how much of the tramway is still visible.

The Haytor granite tramway was ceremoniously opened on 16th September 1820 and was constructed so that stone quarried on Haytor Down could be transported by open, flat-topped, horse-drawn waggons down to Ventiford (Teigngrace). Here, it had then been transferred by crane to canal barges and taken down to the port of Teignmouth, prior to being transported in sea-going vessels to its final destination.

Continue to follow the tramway until, after about 400 metres, you arrive at a junction where a branch of the tramway doubles back to the right. Follow this track into the old workings. At the end of this stretch of track you will be facing back towards the car park. Take the track to the right that climbs back up the hill (between the quarry and the three trees) as this will take you into the most interesting part of the quarry. A track joins from the left and leads to a gate through the fenced enclosure. Go through this gate and follow the track to the left to find Haytor Ponds. You are now in the quarry itself; please hold on to any young children as there are some steep cliffs here.

Haytor Ponds

This quarry was opened in 1819 and at the height of its operation employed up to around 100 men. Much of the granite extracted here, together with that from the other quarries on Haytor Down, was sent away to London, where it was used on the western face and for the flagstones of London Bridge and in the construction of various buildings that included the British Museum, the National Gallery, the Old General Post Office and the Waltham Monument in Ludgate Circus. The quarry was last used in 1919, when stone was taken from here for the Exeter War Memorial. Still visible here are the relics of some heavy winding gear and a crane probably installed at the time the quarry opened.

Relics of the crane, Haytor Quarry
(Author)

These ponds, situated in a beautifully tranquil spot, have in times past been stocked with goldfish, although I have yet to see any! The waters are also a haven for frogs and other wildlife.

Retrace your steps out of the quarry and follow the track straight ahead. Shortly, another grassy track veers off to the left. Take this track and it will lead you straight back to the Haytor lower car park, but before doing so spare a moment to look at the ruined walls and old gatepost near the three trees mentioned earlier - this is now all that remains of a small village where cottages for some of the quarry workers once stood, together with workshops, a pub and a little school.

5. Holne Village and Horseshoe Falls

Start and finish point: SX 706 695.
Distance: 2 km.
Degree of difficulty: *** Mixed terrain, with a tarmac road, a forest track, fields and three stiles which require two adults for easy negotiation.
Brief description: This walk starts and finishes in the delightful village of Holne. The short but challenging route is worth the effort for the fine views of the Double Dart valley and the Horseshoe Falls. You may also reward yourself with refreshments in the village at the end of the walk!

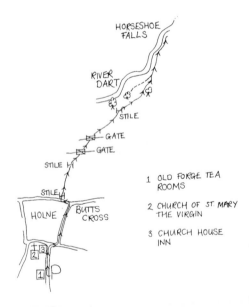

1 OLD FORGE TEA ROOMS

2 CHURCH OF ST MARY THE VIRGIN

3 CHURCH HOUSE INN

Parking is available in the village hall car park (please note the sign to users at the entrance). Leave the car park and join the road. Straight ahead of you is the building that used to house the Old Forge Tea Rooms.

The Old Forge Tea Rooms was once used as a set for a film starring Alastair Sim, John Standing and Harold Pinter. The film, 'Rogue Male', was made in 1976.

Next door to the former Old Forge Tea Rooms, and set back from the road, is the Church of St. Mary the Virgin. This church has a rich history and is worth exploring. For pushchair access walk to the crossroads and turn left past the Church House Inn (which I shall mention later). Then take to a pathway between the inn and Churchway Cottage (formerly the village post office and stores), as this leads to a side gateway to the churchyard.

St. Mary's Church, Holne

The church dates from c.AD 1300 and was enlarged to its present size some 200 years later.
The beautifully carved wooden rood screen in front of the altar has been described as probably being the finest example of a painted screen in the county and features no less than forty painted panels. These depict, in the centre, Christ in glory crowning the Blessed Virgin Mary - supported by an angel and the virgin Saint Cecilia respectively - and, on either side, eighteen saints and martyrs.
The North window is in memoriam to the author Charles Kingsley, who was born in the vicarage in 1819; his father was the curate-in-charge at this time.

Leave the churchyard by the side entrance and head back to the road. Turn right on reaching it and almost immediately turn left at the crossroads, signposted for Ashburton and Princetown. Follow this road to the next junction; the signpost is marked Butts Cross. Turn left here and look for a wooden finger-post on your right marked 'Footpath Newbridge' and carrying the initials 'MW' which stand for Mariners' Way, an ancient coast to coast route between Bideford and Dartmouth. (This is the path you will now follow to the River Dart and the Horseshoe Falls.) Negotiate the first stile carefully - in my experience it is easier and safer to take your child out of the pushchair and carry him or her over the stile before lifting the pushchair over.

Before long a second stile is reached and, beyond it, the path leads you across a field. On reaching the far side of the field, go through the five-bar gate into another field, but remember to shut the gate carefully behind you as these fields are home to horses and donkeys. The area close to this gate, incidentally, may be muddy, and for a short distance beyond it you need to take extra care as there are a number of tree roots protruding from the ground.

When you have reached the far side of this second field go through another gate and then pause for a moment to admire the views over this part of the Double Dart valley. On a clear day you should be able to pick out the southernmost tip of Dr Blackall's Drive (featured in chapter 7) as it curves around the hillside directly opposite from where you are standing, while just beyond it, a little to the left, is the distinctive profile of Sharp Tor. In good visibility Buckland Beacon may also be seen far around to the right (north-east), although from here it appears to be no more than a pimple on the distant skyline.

Once you are ready to continue, follow the clearly-defined grass track diagonally across what is the last of the fields until reaching the final stile of the outward journey. After going over the stile carefully, you will quickly be made aware by a metal sign that you are now on National Trust land and in Holne Woods. From hereon simply follow the track downhill through the woodland - listening out for the rush of the waters of the River Dart and carrying straight on past the point where another track joins the main track from the left - until the Horseshoe Falls are reached on your left-hand side. This a lovely spot for picnics and a rest, however children will need close supervision in such close proximity to the water.

Charles Kingsley, who you may remember was born in Holne Vicarage, was an author whose works included 'The Water Babies'. This novel about a chimney sweep who enters an underwater world richly describes a river's course. Whilst taking in the Horseshoe Falls it is easy to imagine such a place. The following quote finds Tom the chimney sweep exploring his new environment:-

> *...everything is going to the sea, and I will go too...And now, down the rushing stream, past tall birch-fringed rocks which shone out one moment as clear as day, and the next were as dark as night; past dark hovers under swirling banks...on through narrow strids and roaring cataracts, where Tom was deafened and blinded for a moment by the rushing waters; along deep reaches...past sleeping villages; under dark bridge-arches, and away and away to the sea.*

This point marks the furthest part of the walk. A short distance from the Horseshoe Falls and further along the track is Newbridge, with its adjacent car park, toilet facilities and, often, refreshment van. However, reaching these facilities entails negotiation of a

Horseshoe Falls (Author)

kissing gate, stepping-stones and the very narrow and busy bridge itself. I would not advise this with a pushchair. Instead, return to Holne retracing the same route taken out to the falls. The short climb up the hill may be rewarded on your return to Holne by a visit to the Church House Inn, which has a reputation for fine food and which extends a warm welcome to families.

The Church House Inn, Holne

The earliest parts of the Church House Inn date back to 1329, but over the years it has been extended and modernised to become the building that it is today. A writer in the 'Western Morning News' of 21st April 1939 was astonished that the Church House Inn brewed 'Church Ale' - the proceeds from the sale of which went to church funds.

It is alleged that Oliver Cromwell stayed here during the Battle of Totnes in the Civil War, although this cannot be substantiated.

6. Shipley Bridge and Avon Dam

Start and finish point: SX 681 629.
Distance: 6 km.
Degree of difficulty: * Very easy terrain throughout.
Brief description: This easy stroll along a tarmac track should entice even the most inexperienced walker onto the moor and embraces many historical features of Dartmoor's past, which should inspire young and old alike.

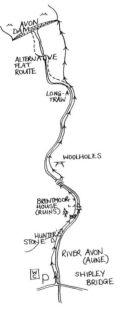

For the most part this walk follows the tarmac road that runs alongside the River Avon, or Aune to give it its correct name. You will find the start of this road at the entrance to the car park - follow it upstream.

You will have noticed the ruins of several buildings around the car park. These had originally been part of a naphtha (peat oil) and peat charcoal works, the peat being extracted from Red Lake Mire and then transported down to Shipley along the three-mile Zeal Tor tramroad. However, by 1850 the operating company formed by L. H. Davy and Wm. Wilkins of Totnes only some three years earlier had failed. Later, around 1872, the buildings had been renovated and modified by another company in connection with the working of china clay at Petre's Pits. Once again, though, the undertaking had soon proved unsuccessful, and the remains that are to be seen nowadays are mostly of the settling tanks where the clay, brought down from the moor, had been refined.

Continue to follow the road as it climbs gently uphill, still following the course of the River Avon.

Approximately 400 metres from the car park a small side road running off and back to the left leads to a water filtration plant. At the junction of the two roads you will see a large inscribed rock known as the 'Hunters' Stone'. This dates back to the late 19th century and was commissioned as a memorial to celebrated local huntsmen by a one-time occupier of Brent Moor House, the ruins of which you will encounter in a short while.

A little further on there is a metal gate across the road: there is no need to open the gate as there is ample room to skirt round it to the left. This gate denotes a noticeable change in vegetation and is, in fact, the entrance to what used to be the Brent Moor House estate. Not far beyond the gate you will come across what is left of the house.

Some of the remains of Brent Moor House

Brent Moor House was built in the early part of the 19th century as a fine gentleman's residence and was originally the home of the Meynell family for many years. Later, in the late-Victorian period, the property became occupied by Mr C. A. Mohun-Harris (a keen hunt-supporter and the instigator of the 'Hunters' Stone'), and remained in use as a private residence until around the outbreak of the Second World War. After being used, briefly, as a youth hostel, it was last occupied in the 1950s, when it served as a dormitory for the water board during the construction of the Avon Dam.

The property then fell into disuse, became more and more delapidated and was eventually demolished in 1968.

After passing through the Brent Moor House estate, the road takes you out onto a more open stretch of moorland and over a bridge. This is a lovely place for a picnic and, indeed, 20 metres or so on the right-hand side there is a picnic bench.

The area directly behind the picnic bench is called 'Woolholes'. In 1848 granite from a quarry here known as Woolla Quarry was sourced for use in the construction of the South Devon Railway between Totnes and Plymouth.

The Avon Dam (Author)

The road continues up the valley and after 600 metres or so you will have your first glimpse of the dam. Soon you will also see a track rising off to the right. For an easy stroll you may continue up the tarmac road to the base of the Avon Dam, but for more spectacular views of the valley you have just walked through, and also a view of the reservoir above the dam, take the track to the right; although rough in places, it is well worth the effort. Arriving at the Avon Dam is the furthest point of the walk and a good opportunity to take a breather and admire this feat of engineering.

Taking in the view (Author)

The 265-metre long Avon Dam was constructed in the 1950s, and the water is used to supply the Totnes and the South Hams areas. When the valley was flooded in order to create the reservoir, part of an extensive prehistoric settlement became submerged, as did a fine example of a late-medieval blowing house - complete with leat, launder-bank, wheel pit and tail-race. Its storage capacity, when full, is slightly in excess of 1,500 million litres of water.

When you have finished admiring the Avon Dam and its surroundings, return to the car park by retracing your steps.

As you descend the hill to rejoin the tarmac road, you will notice a stretch of the river marked on your map as 'Long-a-Traw'. It is here that the river enters a miniature canyon, about which William Crossing, in his 'Guide to Dartmoor', tells us a story:-

It was over this [canyon] that the daring John Dill leaped his horse when pursued by the farmers, from one of whom he had 'borrowed' the animal without going through the form of asking whether he might have it, for the purpose of conveying certain goods that had been quietly landed by night from a village near the coast into the interior.

Crossing fails to mention whether or not Mr Dill outran the farmers to deliver his contraband!

7. Mel Tor and Dr Blackall's Drive

Start and finish point: SX 695 731.
Distance: 4 km.
Degree of difficulty: *** Very little uphill, but some stony/rough terrain.
Brief description: Predominantly level, this walk takes in some spectacular views of the Double Dart valley.

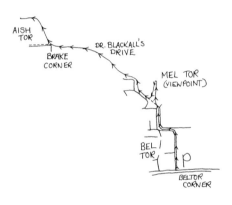

Park in the Bel Tor Corner car park and set off along the track that runs parallel with the enclosure wall. At times this track is not easy to define, but if you keep the wall to your left you will not go astray. At the bottom of the gentle slope, turn left and join the very stony track between two enclosures. Follow this track as it zig-zags towards Mel Tor. (The surface of this track may appear to be too rough for a pushchair, however if one takes a little time and care it is entirely possible.)

When you emerge from between the walls of the enclosures, at the end of what is known as Miltor Lane, Mel Tor is a short walk up the slope in front of you. Pick out a route to the top between the gorse bushes. It is sometimes the case on Dartmoor that leaving the path provides easier terrain for the All-Terrain Pushchair - that would seem to be the case here; you will, in any event, find this quite an easy ascent and the view from the top more than worth the effort.

Mel Tor - or to use its historically correct name, Mil Tor - stands 600 feet above the valley floor and provides a spectacular view of the Double Dart valley.

One of the old Dartmoor customs was the 'Rolling of the Wagon Wheels on Midsummer Day', which took place here. The aim was for the wheels to reach the river, though few ever did. This event was discontinued in the last century, during the war, although revived briefly in the 1950s.

Geologically, Mel Tor is proof itself of the erosion of stone by the elements; on its surface are four basins eroded by rainwater.

Mel Tor, with Venford Reservoir in the distance
(Author)

Descend to the track that you previously left, taking care to dodge the gorse bushes. On reaching the track, turn right. You are now on Dr Blackall's Drive.

Dr Blackall lived during the latter half of the 19th century at Spitchwick Manor, near Poundsgate. This track was a 'carriage drive' cut around 1880 by estate worker Gerald Warren and members of his family on Dr Blackall's orders, so that he could take leisurely drives and enjoy the exceptional views.

A short while after rejoining the track, the route bends to the right and again sharply to the left. This short section of track is steep. Keep a tight hold on the pushchair, using the wrist-strap should you have one.

From here you will have a good view of Bench Tor (sometimes known as Benjy Tor) on the opposite side of the valley.

A view of Dr Blackall's Drive, and Mel Tor beyond (Author)

Continue along Dr Blackall's Drive until reaching Brake Corner (you will see the corner of a walled enclosure on your left). The track you are following bears right at this point, skirting around the almost indistinguishable Aish Tor. Before losing too much height, turn around and retrace your steps as this is the furthest point of the walk.

Stop for a few moments to enjoy the view of the valley. Writing in 1920, in his book entitled 'Holne, Dartmoor', the Rev. W. H. Harvey Royse, RN dedicated a chapter to local weather lore. Interestingly the Dart was said to cry when there was to be a change of weather:-

'Us shall have bad weather. I hear the Broadstones a-crying.' (The Broadstones are the large granite boulders which lie on the bed of the river). The reverend does offer

the opinion, however, that this is more than likely the 'piping of the wind in the turnings of the valley combined with the roar of the river'.

Dartmoor has many legends. Another of these relates to Bel Tor, the tor seen inside the enclosure next to the car park. (A better view of this can be enjoyed on the return to the car park.) Bel Tor has a remarkable logan stone with a large rock basin on its surface. The legend says that good fortune awaits anyone seeing the reflection of the rising sun in the water collected in it.

A Brougham carriage, which was a popular mode of transport in the late-19th century, when Dr Blackall's Drive was created.

8. Babeny and Sherwell

Start and finish point: SX 682 739.
Distance: 5 km.
Degree of difficulty: * Easy terrain throughout.
Brief description: A very easy walk that takes in some splendid views and a closer look at two very ancient Dartmoor settlements.

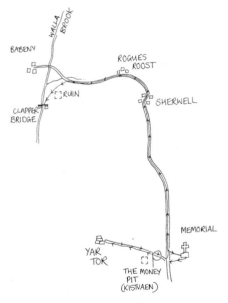

Park just off the 'Sherwell and Babeny' road, on the plateau between the memorial cross on the right-hand side of the road and Yar Tor on the left-hand side of the road. Then take the clearly-defined grassy track that ascends from where you parked to the top of Yar Tor. A short distance from your car, and by the side of the track, you will see the remains of a prehistoric burial chamber, or kist-vaen.

This burial chamber has for many years been known locally as 'The Money Pit'. The story goes that a local farmer, Edward Caunter, had a dream that the chamber contained treasure. He awoke the next day determined to find it, but on exploring the ruins he was disappointed to find nothing apart from a heart-shaped piece of flint. However, on taking this home he became a changed man - morose and bad-tempered - until some months later his son found the flint in a

37

cupboard, took it for a plaything and left it somewhere on the moor. The farmer then became warm-hearted again and realised, when he found it missing, that possessing the 'Heart of Flint' had changed his nature.

Continue up the track to the summit cairn on Yar Tor. It is well worth the effort because from this vantage point the views are outstanding, particularly of Sharp Tor and the East Dart valley above Dartmeet. Further afield, a vast expanse of central Dartmoor can also be seen, the only blot on the landscape being the television mast on North Hessary Tor, over six miles away to the west.

After you have surveyed this wonderful scenery, return to the spot from where you first set off, turn left and follow the road downhill. (Although this road leads only to Sherwell and Babeny, and is relatively little used, please bear in mind that it is, nevertheless, still a highway and that you need to keep an eye out for approaching traffic.) Soon you will see a number of old enclosures to the left, and it is just below these that the road will eventually lead you to the first of the dwellings comprising the tiny hamlet of Sherwell.

Higher Sherwell and Hornet's Castle

The name 'Sherwell' means 'clear spring', and during the early part of the 19th century the farmer living in the house that you have just reached, Higher Sherwell, used it as an ale-house and as a venue for cock-fighting, calling it 'The Cocklers' Peep Inn'. It was also around this time that the unusually-shaped thatched building to the right of the road known as Hornet's Castle, which had originally been built as a labourer's cottage for Middle Sherwell, was the home of a certain Dorothea ('Dolly') Trebble. Previously she and her husband, William, had lived with their children at 'Dolly's Cot' (the ruins of which are situated on the west bank of the nearby East Dart River), and later another of their homes included Swincombe Cottage - better known as 'Dolly Trebble's House' and mentioned in the next chapter.

Immediately behind Higher Sherwell, and visible from just a little further along the road, are several buildings that make up a farm. This is Middle Sherwell, where the original farmhouse is so old that it was built before the introduction of fireplaces and staircases. Even the more recent farmhouse, a longhouse built at right-angles to its still-surviving predecessor, is said to be at least 400 years old!

Follow the road as it weaves through Sherwell and carry on to the next group of buildings, situated on the right-hand side and known as Rogues Roost.

The comparatively recent dwelling here stands on the site of a former longhouse, West Sherwell, which was once used as a centre for sheep rustling, hence the name Rogues Roost. Another interesting tale regarding the earlier dwelling concerns 'Granny West' - reputedly a white witch - who kept her 'mad' teenage son prisoner in an outhouse until a passer-by alerted the authorities.

Just beyond Rogues Roost the road passes between ancient field hedges, and here, in summer, the scent of wild honeysuckle fills the air. The downhill gradient now also starts to steepen, and soon you will hear the waters of a stream which passes underneath the road. However, just before reaching this spot you need to look out for a wooden finger-post on the left-hand side marked 'Public Bridleway': it is, in fact, situated immediately above a passing place for vehicles and not far from where the road terminates at

Babeny - one of the ancient tenements of the Forest of Dartmoor.

Babeny Clapper Bridge (Author)

Leave the road here, turning off to the left, and follow the footpath as best you can. Initially, there are a few rocks to negotiate, but after a very short distance you will reach a beautiful spot for a picnic in a wide grassy area near the stream. Follow the stream downhill, picking up the path again as you approach the trees; this will shortly lead you to a fairy-like clapper bridge. (Some of the terrain here is a little uneven, with roots and rocks.) Once you have enjoyed this area, return to the road by the same route, turn right and retrace your steps to the starting point of the walk.

As you approach your car, a short detour can be made to look at a more recent monument. Opposite your car you should find a track to the left, which will take you to a cross atop a small rock pile.

The Cave-Penney Memorial

This cross, known as Sherwell Cross, is to the memory of Evelyn Anthony Cave-Penney who was killed by a sniper in Palestine on June 8th 1918, at the age of 19. The rock underneath it is known as the 'Belstone Bible'.

9. The Swincombe Valley

Start and finish point: SX 651 728.

Distance: 4 km.

Degree of difficulty: ** Mostly very easy terrain, but waterlogged in parts after heavy rain.

Brief description: For the most part this walk is on good tracks and a metalled road. There are many interesting features to see, all telling of man's relationship with Dartmoor. Among them are a disused leat, bridges, ruined houses, beehives and the remains of an old tin mine.

The starting point for this walk is alongside the lane leading to Sherberton, which is a 'no through road' that commences at a junction on the Holne - Hexworthy road just above the Forest Inn. Drive along this lane for about 600 metres, passing a track (signposted 'Public Bridlepath') going off to the left between two walls, and park on the right-hand side of the lane just before reaching a gate. After leaving your car, walk back along the lane until you reach the 'Public Bridlepath' sign and then join the track, which soon bears around to the right. At this point it begins to run just below, and parallel to, the Wheal Emma Leat channel.

The Wheal Emma Leat was taken in from the River Swincombe near Foxtor Mire in 1859 and cut as an artificial waterway contouring around the hillsides of the open moorland for a distance of over 15 kilometres. Its purpose was to augment the supply of water from the River Mardle to drive the wheels of a 19th century copper mine - Wheal Emma - situated to the north-west of Buckfastleigh in Brook Wood, a role that it fulfilled for around 50 years.

Continue to follow the track across the open moorland. As you start to lose height on the hill, notice a stone wall approximately 100 metres away to your right, running parallel with the track. There are two stones which appear larger than the rest. Leave the track and head towards these. Although a little bumpy underfoot, it is still possible to take the pushchair across this stretch of the moor.

The large upright stones are part of the remains of Swincombe Cottage (better known as Dolly Trebble's House) and formed the jambs of the fireplace. According to William Crossing, in his 'Guide to Dartmoor', these stones could have been door jambs removed from a hut circle higher up the hill, but he gives no indication of when this may have occurred. However, it is known that around the mid-19th century this was another of the dwellings occupied by 'Dolly' Trebble (see chapter 8). Often referred to as something of a beauty, she and her family lived here for a short while before moving into a cottage at Prince Hall.

Fairy Bridge

Return to the main track. Turn right along it and continue downhill. The River Swincombe shortly comes into view - spanned by Fairy Bridge, to where you are now heading. As the track drops down onto the metalled road it becomes quite rough. You may find it easier to skirt to the right to find a suitable way down.

This beautiful, tranquil spot holds many clues to man's long connection with Dartmoor. The three traditional methods of crossing the river are found next to each other - ford, stepping-stones and bridge.

Across the bridge, and to the right, is a former homestead. It is known both as Lower Swincombe

The doorway of John Bishop's House

and, more widely, as John Bishop's House. Bishop was an expert drystone wall builder and the unusual porch, with its three stepped granite blocks, is testament to his skill.

To the left of John Bishop's House and, further upstream, are the ruins of Higher Swincombe, the impressive gateposts of which are still clearly visible. This building was one of the lodges erected by Sir Thomas Tyrwhitt of Tor Royal.

After exploring the relics of Dartmoor's past, return to the road and head left (north-eastwards) along it. At this point the river is almost alongside the road, but soon they start to diverge and Gobbet Plain

Gatepost, Higher Swincombe (Author)

opens out before you. This, and the area above the road, is the site of a former tin mine. The road, meanwhile, now bears sharp right and the bank drops away quite steeply towards the river. If you stop and look closely here you will find the remains of some millstones.

The millstones are large round granite blocks with smaller round hollows at their centre, and the remains here include both the upper and lower stones of an ore-grinding, or crazing, mill.

A millstone (Author)

Further along the plain are the remains of a large pit that would have contained a waterwheel, and also a mine building that was once used as a 'counting house'.

On the opposite side of the river, in a small enclosure, are the beehives belonging to the monks of Buckfast Abbey, where Buckfast honey is harvested.

Return to the road and continue to follow it in an easterly direction until you reach a gate.

To the right of the road can be seen a granite 'entrance'. This contains a pipeline which carries water from Swincombe Reservoir to Venford Reservoir. The structure was formerly an adit of Gobbet Tin Mine.

Go through the gate, remembering to shut it behind you, and follow the lane up the hill until you reach the spot where you parked your car.

10. Hound Tor and Greator Rocks

Start and finish point: SX 739 792.
Distance: 3 km.
Degree of difficulty: ** Moderately challenging, with some rough and uphill terrain.
Brief description: A ramble over open moorland that takes in one of Dartmoor's best-known tors and the extensive remains of a medieval village. This walk also provides the opportunity for you to enjoy a variety of far-reaching views in every direction.

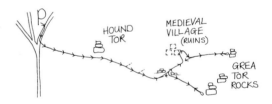

Park your car in the large car park just off the Swallerton Gate road junction. On leaving the car, turn back towards the crossroads. At the junction turn left onto the open moorland, following the broad green track heading up the right-hand side of Hound Tor. Make your way to the top of this incline; you are aiming to pass to the right of the tor and thus avoid the boulder-strewn outcrop.

The rocks which form Hound Tor are steeped in Dartmoor legend and one cannot help but be impressed by their imposing outline. Some say that this silhouette was created by a coven of angry witches, who were upset by a local huntsman called Bowerman when he unintentionally disturbed their activities whilst galloping across the moor with his hounds. Bowerman's fate was sealed when the witches turned him to stone - the so-called Bowerman's

Nose on nearby Hayne Down. Bowerman's hounds allegedly met a similar end here on Hound Tor, and it is said that their petrified shapes form the outline of the tor. Perhaps a little far-fetched, although a man called Bowerman did live near Hound Tor at the time of William the Conqueror!

From Hound Tor, looking across to
Haytor Rocks (Author)

Facing south-eastwards, and keeping the distant Haytor Rocks almost directly in front of you, continue to follow the grassy track - indistinct at first - away from Hound Tor. As you walk away from the outcrop look carefully for tracks turning off to the left. Take the third and most distinct of these, which will lead you downhill towards the remains of the medieval village.

As you continue walking downhill, these remains appear as a series of distinct chambers with connecting passageways and are well worthy of a closer inspection. However, to do this means eventually leaving the track and making a slight deviation over terrain that is somewhat rough in places and inhospitable to the pushchair. I would strongly suggest, therefore, that the pushchair should be left anchored at a convenient point off the track and that you carry your child carefully over the short distance involved.

Remains of Hundatora village
with Hound Tor behind

The medieval village of 'Hundatora' was abandoned at some time during the 14th century, possibly due to the spread of the 'Black Death' which decimated the population of Devon. Originally settled in the 10th century, this village latterly included four farmhouses and three barns which would have been used for drying corn. Excavation suggests that the thick stone walls would have been topped with turf, straw, heather or rushes.

Having explored the ruins, return to the track that brought you to this point. Turn left now, heading towards the lowest pile of Greator Rocks. This outcrop, slightly detached from the rest of this imposing tor, is a wonderful viewpoint for looking back towards Hound Tor. Keen eyes may spot buzzards circling above the valley.

Retrace your steps down towards the remains of the medieval village, and then continue up the hill towards the crest of the ridge between Hound Tor and Grea Tor. At the point where a wall crosses this track, turn left and walk to the right-hand side of Grea Tor. Looking in a south-easterly direction, you will have a superb view of Holwell Tor across Houndtor Coombe - the valley below.

Walk back to the wall/track junction, turn left and head uphill again. Soon afterwards turn right onto the grassy track back towards Hound Tor and, keeping the tor on your right, follow this all the way back to the crossroads before turning right and returning to your car.

Hound Tor, as seen from the car park (Author)

11. Bellever Forest

Start and finish point: SX 656 771.
Distance: 5 km.
Degree of difficulty: * Easy terrain throughout.
Brief description: Bellever Forest provides many opportunities for getting out with the pushchair, some routes being waymarked by the Forestry Commission which manages the area. I have chosen a route that takes in forest, far-reaching moorland views, an interesting ruin and a walk through a working farm.

Park your car in the main Forestry Commission car park just to the west of Bellever Bridge. Here you will find a toilet block complete with a superb baby-changing facility located inside the disabled toilet.

Join the track that runs through the car park and set off in a southerly direction, noting the picnic areas on either side. Soon you will reach a gate. Go through this and continue to follow the track as it starts to rise until you reach the point where it forks; take the right-hand fork signed 'Laughter Hole Farm'.

Continue to follow the track up the slope. You will eventually reach a gateway which marks the entrance to the farm. Pause by the gate and look to your left, towards the opposite side of the valley. You should be able to see a large enclosure with smaller enclosures inside it. If you look closely you will also be able to make out the remains of a building; this was 'Snaily House'.

The story of Snaily House and how it came by its unusual name is best told by William Crossing in his 'Guide to Dartmoor' :-

> *Two spinsters who dwelt here aroused the curiosity of the few gossips in the sparsely populated neighbourhood by their mysterious way of living. They never did any work in the garden, nor had they any cattle, and no food was ever seen to be taken to the house. Yet they always presented a buxom appearance. At length it was discovered that they subsisted on black slugs, which they gathered on the moor. The secret being out the women pined and died, and the dwelling fell to ruin.*

Go through the farm gate. There are usually lots of horses to see in these paddocks to the left and right of the track. As you walk on there is also a fantastic view of this secluded valley.

A view of the East Dart valley from near Laughter Hole Farm

The East Dart valley is home to much wildlife, and you may well see buzzards, sparrowhawks and goldcrests. Interestingly the stretch of the river that runs through Bellever is one of the most significant spawning sites for Atlantic Salmon in the whole River Dart catchment area.

Pass through the enclosures of Laughter Hole Farm and, on reaching the gate at the far end, go through and take the right-hand track up the hill.

The original farmstead - not one of the ancient tenements of the Forest of Dartmoor - was located lower down the hill than the present-day bungalow.

On Christmas Day 1923 an earthquake tremor was felt in this area. The tenant of Laughter Hole Farm at the time, Mr Stephens, was quoted as saying: "Pictures were swinging to and fro on the wall, and holly and paper decorations fell down. Everything seemed to be on the shake." Hard to imagine in such a quiet spot!

The remains of the earlier settlement

At the top of the short, steep climb, the open moor can be glimpsed straight ahead. There is a bench here and it is a suitable spot to stop for a breather. On regaining your composure, turn back in the direction from whence you came and take the left-hand fork. This elevated track gives you a superb view out onto the open moorland, and serves as a reminder that this coniferous forest is in sharp contrast to the natural vegetation of Dartmoor.

Afforestation began at Bellever in the 1930s and more or less coincided with the demise of a great annual event on the Dartmoor hunting calendar - 'Bellever Day'. Normally held on a Friday in April, this would attract people to Bellever Tor from all over the moor and William Crossing, mentioning the 1901 event in his work entitled 'A Hundred Years on Dartmoor', states 'that fully a thousand persons were present, more than five hundred of them being mounted, while vehicles of every description were to be seen on the slopes around the tor'. It must have been quite an occasion!

Eventually the track on which you are now walking loses height and comes to a junction. Follow the track hard right as this will drop you back to a point near the first gate of Laughter Hole Farm. Turn left here and follow this track back to the car park. If you look through the trees to your left you should be able to glimpse Bellever Tor on the horizon.

Before returning to your car, I can recommend a short diversion to see the beautiful 13th century clapper bridge. After passing to the right of the toilet block, follow a short trail down to the river, turn left where there is a small post to your right marked with a wheelchair and walk along the riverbank. On reaching the bridge, either retrace your steps along the riverbank to return to your car or walk along the road and then turn left at the entrance to the car park.

Bellever bridges (Author)

12. Nun's Cross I

Start and finish point: SX 590 735.
Distance: 8 km.
Degree of difficulty: ** Easy terrain, with moderate uphill sections.
Brief description: Starting from Princetown, this walk is relatively long, but the going is easy, there are fine views to enjoy and much to be seen of a historical nature.

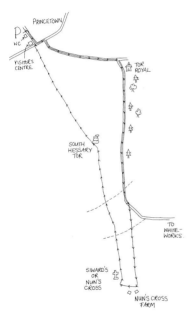

Park in the centre of Princetown, in the car park adjacent to the High Moorland Visitor Centre in Tavistock Road, and walk along the pavement in front of this building towards The Plume of Feathers. Cross the road carefully opposite the pub, turn left and then turn right into the road which runs alongside the Methodist chapel and leads to Whiteworks. Soon, after following this road gently uphill for a short distance, it will be worth pausing for a moment to look back at what is a superb view of Princetown and its prison.

The prison was essentially completed in 1809 and was built to house French prisoners who had previously been detained on huge decommissioned warships in Plymouth. Later, in 1813, large numbers of Americans captured during the war of 1812 also started being detained here, but conditions were harsh to say the least at this time and many prisoners of both nationalities perished. Those who did survive, though, were eventually repatriated after the wars with America and France came to an end around 1814/15, and in February 1816 the prison became deserted. However in 1850, when the Colonies started refusing to accept any more convicts, the prison was recommissioned for civil prisoners and has continued to fulfil this role ever since. (For more information on this fascinating history I would recommend a visit to the Dartmoor Prison Museum which is located on the Tavistock Road, not far from the prison entrance.)

Princetown (Author)

After about a kilometre follow the road as it bears sharply to the right. On the corner here is Tor Royal, the former home of Sir Thomas Tyrwhitt.

Thomas Tyrwhitt was the founder of Princetown (or Prince's Town, as it was then known) and the holder of many offices which included Private Secretary to the Prince of Wales, Auditor of the Duchy of Cornwall, MP for Okehampton, Portarlington and Plymouth between the years 1796 and 1812, Lord Warden of the Stannaries of Devon and Cornwall, and, on being knighted in 1812, Gentleman Usher of the Black Rod. He was also the instigator of the building of the prison when his 'agricultural plans' failed and, later, played a major role in promoting The Plymouth & Dartmoor Railway (see chapter 15).

Tor Royal dates back to 1785, when Tyrwhitt embarked on an ambitious plan to bring a large area of Dartmoor into cultivation. Although he ultimately failed to achieve his objectives - primarily because of the poverty of the soil and the adverse climate of the area - the task of building the house, erecting several

farm buildings in the neighbourhood and enclosing well over
2,000 acres of moorland was completed in 1798. As Private
Secretary and friend of the Prince Regent it is alleged that Tyrwhitt
entertained the then future monarch (King George IV) here,
although this cannot be substantiated.

Continue to follow the road for approximately two more
kilometres. Then, just after it starts to bend away to the left, leave
the road and take the broad track heading southwards. This track
will lead you directly to Nun's Cross Farm and from it, on a clear
day, you will have a good view of the Whiteworks area to your left
and also, beneath you in the same direction, the infamous Foxtor
Mire.

*This area is most notorious as the setting for the 'Great Grimpen
Mire' in Conan-Doyle's 'The Hound of the Baskervilles' and has
reputedly dragged at least one
escaped convict to his death.*

The track drops you directly into
the old enclosures of Nun's
Cross Farm, and the remains of
the buildings can be seen in front
of you.

*Nun's Cross Farm was enclosed
in about 1870 by John Hooper,
who erected a small thatched
cottage for himself and his wife
to live in. However, the farmhouse that can still be seen is of
later date, having been built to
provide a home for their married
daughter and her husband in
1901. In later years the original*

Sluice-gate on the Devonport
Leat near Nun's Cross Farm

dwelling was used as a shippon and the more modern one was occupied by a succession of other tenants until being vacated at around the time of the Second World War.

The enclosures here provide a good spot for a picnic or a rest. On the western edge of the enclosures you will see Nun's, or Siward's, Cross - the point from which you will later continue the walk. First, however, there is the opportunity to take a small diversion to see some tin workings and the ever beautiful Devonport Leat. The track on which you entered the enclosures becomes indistinct. As it passes through the break in the wall in front of Nun's Cross Farm follow a line towards the junction of the enclosure walls on the side of Crane Hill in front of you. You will soon pick up a more distinct track again, which drops you directly to the leat and amongst some interesting tin workings. Having explored this area, retrace your steps back to the enclosures and, indeed, make your way across them to the cross itself.

Standing at just over two metres high, Siward's Cross is a monument of great antiquity. It was one of the great Abbots' Way series of crosses, and was visited by the 'Knights of the Perambulation' in 1240, recorded at that time as 'Crucem Siwardi'.

Turn right along the track next to the cross, heading away from the cross and back towards Princetown: this track will lead you all the way back to Princetown, past South Hessary Tor. On a fine day this part of the route provides some superb far-reaching views and it can feel as if you are in the middle of nowhere. The track, meanwhile, descends from South Hessary Tor, passes through several enclosure walls and eventually drops you into the car park behind The Plume of Feathers - a good opportunity to rest your tired feet and enjoy some liquid refreshment or a spot of lunch.

For additional information on Whiteworks refer also to the Nun's Cross II walk, a shorter version of this one.

13. Nun's Cross II

Start and finish point: SX 604 708.
Distance: 2 km.
Degree of difficulty: * Easy terrain, with moderate uphill sections.
Brief description: This walk comprises a much shorter route than the previous one for those wishing to visit Nun's Cross. Parking is normally available in one of the small areas just off the road to Whiteworks. (Please note that with consideration of the reader in mind, descriptions common to both routes have been repeated in order to avoid the need for constant page-turning.)

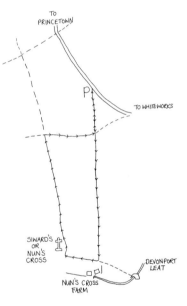

Park your car and take the track that heads southwards. (The road bends away to your left.) This track will lead you directly to Nun's Cross Farm and from it, on a clear day, you will have a good view of the Whiteworks area to your left and also, beneath you in the same direction, the infamous Foxtor Mire.

This area is most notorious as the setting for the 'Great Grimpen Mire' in Conan-Doyle's 'The Hound of the Baskervilles' and has reputedly dragged at least one escaped convict to his death.

Whiteworks was so named because the ore that was mined here produced a 'white' tin after being processed. William Crossing, writing in his famous 'Guide to Dartmoor', states that: 'we remember when two large waterwheels were to be seen revolving here, and when the blacksmith's hammer was constantly heard ringing on the anvil'. The mine itself reached a peak of production in the mid-1870s, which more or less coincided with a London architect being commissioned to draw up plans for cottages for the workers. Unfortunately, though, the mine failed before these dewllings were completed and they were then purchased by the Home Office for married prison warders.

As one would imagine, this area has always been greatly influenced by the presence of the prison in Princetown - in more ways than one! Not far from here is the ruin of a building known as 'Lovey Lee's Snail Farm'. This enterprising old lady was known to collect slugs from the moor during the early part of the 19th century and to sell them at Princetown as a delicacy for the French prisoners.

The track drops you directly into the old enclosures of Nun's Cross Farm, and the remains of the buildings can be seen in front of you.

Nun's Cross Farm was enclosed in about 1870 by John Hooper, who erected a small thatched cottage for himself and his wife to live in. However, the farmhouse that can still be seen is of later date, having been built to provide a home for their married daughter and her husband in 1901. In later years the original dwelling was used as a shippon and the more modern one was occupied by a succession of other tenants until being vacated at around the time of the Second World War.

Tin workings, with Nun's Cross Farm in the distance (Author)

The enclosures here provide a good spot for a picnic or a rest. You will see from here, on the western edge of the enclosures, Nun's, or Siward's, Cross - the point from which you will later continue the walk. First, however, there is the opportunity to take a small diversion to see some tin workings and the ever beautiful Devonport Leat. The track on which you entered the enclosures becomes indistinct. As it passes through the break in the wall in front of Nun's Cross Farm follow a line towards the junction of the enclosure walls on the side of Crane Hill in front of you. You will soon pick up a more distinct track again, which drops you directly to the leat and amongst some interesting tin workings. Having explored this area, retrace your steps back to the enclosures and, indeed, make your way across them to the cross itself.

Nun's, or Siward's, Cross

Standing at just over two metres high, Siward's Cross is a monument of great antiquity. It was one of the great Abbots' Way series of crosses, and was visited by the 'Knights of the Perambulation' in 1240, recorded at that time as 'Crucem Siwardi'.

Turn right along the track next to the cross, heading away from the cross and back towards Princetown. After passing a boundary stone on the left-hand side of the track, walk a further 100 metres or so and turn right at the crossroads next to a large boulder. From there follow this other track until you arrive at a junction with the track on which you first set out on the walk and then turn left to return to your car.

14. Burrator and Crazywell Pool

Start and finish point: SX 569 693.

Distance: 5 km.

Degree of difficulty: * or ** Fairly easy terrain apart from being stony in places, with moderate uphill sections.

Brief description: Extremely picturesque, this walk will enable you to experience the contrast of managed woodlands with open moorland and to enjoy ever-changing views of nearby tors and a stunning reservoir. There are also opportunities to adapt the walk to suit the walkers.

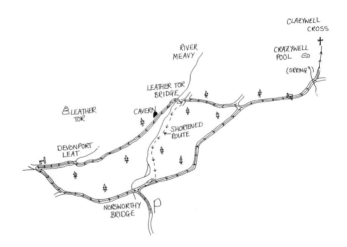

Park in the Norsworthy Bridge car park (marked on the Ordnance Survey map) and set off by heading northwards along the road. At the sharp bend of the road turn right up the forest track. After a short distance the track widens; keep to the right, taking the track between walls and following it uphill. After 800 metres or so the track widens again. Keep to the right along the edge of the forest, heading out towards the open moorland.

Pass through the gateway that marks the end of the plantation on your left. As you continue along the track and round a bend, a cross comes into view on the horizon. This is Crazywell Cross, the furthest point of the walk. (The track now becomes increasingly stony and you are soon entering an area riddled with former tin workings.)

Crazywell Gert (the large gully ahead of you) contains a tributary of Newleycombe Lake and immediately above it lies Crazywell Pool, where the water level is kept fairly constant by a hidden spring. The pool itself is normally about 4.5 metres deep, yet legend has it that the bell ropes of Walkhampton Church, tied end to end and lowered into its depths, did not reach the bottom. Another of several legends attached to this spot is that at dusk and dawn a voice might be heard from the pool calling the name of the next person in the neighbourhood to die.

On the far side of Crazywell Gert a track veers off to the left. Follow this track carefully up the hill; it will lead you to Crazywell Cross, from where a fine view can be had down the valley.

This cross - once sited further down the hill - formed part of the Abbots' Way series of crosses, marking the route taken by the monks across the moor.

Return to the track and retrace your steps to the edge of the plantation from where you emerged earlier. As you enter the plantation again it is worth noting that on your right-hand side, not far above the track, lie the remains of Roundy Farm dating from around 1668, although it is believed that the farm building was erected on the site of an even earlier dwelling. Continue along the track until reaching the wide junction noted on the way up earlier. Turn right and then left onto another wide and sometimes stony track. Walking through the forest, you are now heading for Leather Tor Bridge.

Leather Tor Bridge

Leather Tor Bridge was built in the 1830s as a clapper of two openings and is a very picturesque spot. If one looks carefully seven of the 'Riddipit Steps' (stepping-stones) can still be seen, as can the overgrown Bronze Age ford.

Cross the bridge and follow the track - itself part of the Abbots' Way - as it runs parallel to the River Meavy. A little further on, to your right, you will see a cavern in the bank next to the track. This cavern was once used by the local farmers for the storage of potatoes.

The track emerges from the plantation to reveal the slopes of Leather Tor on the right and almost immediately crosses the Devonport Leat by means of an iron bridge - take care as this may be slippery.

The Devonport Leat was engineered in the late 18th century to provide a new supply of water for the town of Dock (or Devonport,

Cross at Cross Gates, with Burrator Lake in the distance (Author)

as it is now called). At the time there had been a huge growth of the dockyard and related industries, and the population had also increased in line with this.

Continue to follow the track until it reaches the metalled road. Before turning left onto the road, take a moment to soak up the superb view - bench provided! - towards Burrator Reservoir.

The reservoir was created in order to increase the quantity and to improve the quality of Plymouth's water supply. It was officially opened on 21st September 1898, but was then enlarged to its present-day capacity by raising the height of the two dams by three metres, a task that took over four years - between 1923 and 1928 - to complete. At that time the Sheepstor road was carried over the valley by a temporary suspension bridge.

Unfortunately, when a project as large as Burrator Reservoir is undertaken, it is inevitable that there is a price to pay. That price was the submersion of much history. Farms in the catchment area also had to be abandoned, even if they were not submerged, and, as a result, fell into ruin. Trees were planted and the area immediately around the reservoir became the managed forest that it is today.

Turn left and follow the metalled road downhill. You will no doubt enjoy, as we did, being on a smooth road again! At the bottom of the hill the road joins the main road that circumnavigates the reservoir. Turn left and follow this road back to the car park, taking care to look out for traffic.

15. King's Tor and Two Quarries

Start and finish point: SX 568 750.

Distance: 7 km.

Degree of difficulty: ** Some stony/rough sections, but otherwise easy and almost level terrain. (Please take care and supervise children in the vicinity of the quarries.)

Brief description: Taking in two quarries and with wide-ranging views, this walk along disused railway tracks reveals glimpses of Dartmoor's industrial past that have helped to shape the architecture of our capital. This area of Dartmoor provided the stone that was used in the building of some of London's most well-known landmarks.

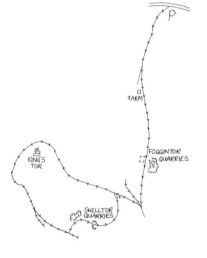

Park in the small lay-by adjacent to the track leading to Yellowmeade Farm, as this track forms the first part of the walk. After approximately 800 metres the track forks; keep to the left-hand track which runs above Yellowmeade Farm and start looking out for the tell-tale signs of the remains of a railway line underfoot.

This railway line was once part of The Plymouth and Dartmoor Railway, a horse-drawn tramroad that wound its way up on to the moor from Sutton Pool (Plymouth) to Princetown. Completed in the 1820s, it had been promoted by Sir Thomas Tyrwhitt (the founder of Princetown) as an integral part of a somewhat over-ambitious scheme to bring renewed prosperity to Princetown following the closure of the prison in 1816. Tyrwhitt's idea was that the railway could be used to bring such commodities as lime and sea sand into the area to aid in the cultivation of parts of the moor, and that products from the moor - flax, hemp, peat and granite etc - could be transported down to the quays at Plymouth. However, most of his plans went unfulfilled, and the main use to which the tramroad was put was for the transportation of granite extracted from the quarries opened hereabouts on Walkhampton Common.

After passing the field enclosures belonging to the farm, you will soon reach Foggintor Quarry. Still visible is the dramatic ruin of the quarry manager's dwelling and, below it, the remains of the cottages which would have housed some of the quarry workers. (None of these structures are entirely stable, so explore with caution and supervise children closely.)

The remains of the quarry manager's dwelling,
Foggintor Quarry

Foggintor Quarry was opened in about 1820 and reached a peak of production in the 1840s, when it employed a workforce of around 300. It eventually closed down in 1906 after having yielded many thousands of tons of granite which was used for a variety of purposes, including the building of Nelson's Column.

After exploring the quarry, continue along the track until reaching a junction of several tracks. Turn right here and join the clearly-defined track that contours around the hillside towards King's Tor. This was formerly the trackbed of another part of The Plymouth & Dartmoor Railway as well as that of its successor - the Princetown Railway (later part of the Great Western Railway system), which ran from Yelverton to Princetown during the years 1883 to 1956. (Do not be tempted to take to the track that rises up to King's Tor itself, but remain on this broad track which provides almost level walking.)

Below King's Tor can be found evidence of a prehistoric settlement consisting of a Bronze Age pound and a number of hut circles, one even with door jambs still visible. On nearby Long Ash Common there are also several standing stones and what are often collectively referred to as the Merrivale antiquities, including the well-known double stone rows. According to William Crossing, in his 'Guide to Dartmoor', this last group of remains was formerly known in the neighbourhood as the Plague Market or Potato Market. He adds that 'a tradition stated that provisions were brought here by the country people and deposited as supplies for Tavistock, at a time [1625] when the plague ravaged that town'.

The corbels, Swell Tor Quarry (Author)

Continue to follow the track around King's Tor, through a cutting. Then, as you come round to the north-western side of the tor, you will find yourself overlooking the River Walkham in the valley below and also be able to see, high up on the opposite side, Dartmoor's tallest outcrop - Vixen Tor - which is currently (2005) at the centre of an access dispute. The track, meanwhile, forks a little further on, and it is here that you need to take the left-hand, higher track heading towards Swell Tor Quarry. Shortly after this junction you will come across a number of corbels at the side of the track.

These granite corbels, cut in 1903 from Swell Tor Quarry and placed in a row at the siding, were made for the widening of London Bridge, but were surplus to requirements. However, when the bridge was later being dismantled in the 1960s, prior to being shipped block by block to Arizona, one of the corbels broke and was replaced by one of the spares from here.

The track gets a little rocky underfoot from hereon, but is easily managed if you take your time: you are now, in fact, entering Swell Tor Quarry which, it is believed, was last operated in 1937. There are remains of a building - the former blacksmith's shop - on the right-hand side of the track, and if you look though the two windows, you will have a fantastic view out to the Tamar estuary.

Shortly beyond the building the track splits again. Take the left-hand, upper track and follow this all the way around the hill, as it will lead you back to the junction below Foggintor Quarry. From there, retrace your steps towards Foggintor Quarry, past Yellowmeade Farm and eventually back to your car.

Part of the ruined building near the entrance to Swell Tor Quarry (Author)

16. Brent Tor

Start and finish point: SX 469 806.

Distance: 6 km.

Degree of difficulty: ** An initial steep, but short, climb. Otherwise mainly easy terrain (much of the route consists of roadways), with moderate uphill sections.

Brief description: Brent Tor sits right on the perimeter of Dartmoor and this walk has a very different feel to that of other walks in this book.

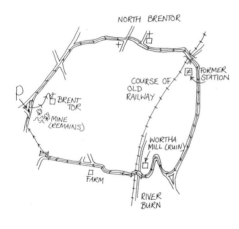

Park in the Brent Tor car park, where you will find picnic benches and toilet facilities, and join the path directly opposite the gate that leads up to the Church of St. Michael de Rupe (of the Rock). (Take care crossing the road.) Twenty metres or so from where the track leaves the wall (on the right), take the grassy track between banks on your left - this provides a pushchair-friendly route up to the church.

The Church of St. Michael of the Rock stands on what was believed to be a volcanic cone. The first church here was built in about 1130, and there are several variations of a legend attached to it. In one, it is said that the Devil himself intervened in the building of the church, moving the stones each night to hamper progress. The people of the village then prayed to St. Michael who, in answer, hid behind Cox Tor one night and threw a great rock at the Devil, driving him away.

Christ Church, North Brentor

After admiring the spectacular views from the church, retrace your steps to the road and turn right along it. The next section of the walk is along this moderately busy road. PLEASE EXERCISE CAUTION, walking towards the oncoming traffic and in single file.

Continue along the road until you reach the second turning to the right signposted Brentor and Mary Tavy. Follow this road downhill as it drops into the village. On entering the village, pass the old chapel on the right and, at the war memorial, turn right, heading towards the church.

The church in this small hamlet of North Brentor is called Christ Church and is a 'chapel-of-ease' to the parish church of St. Michael. Opposite the church is a delightful fenced garden with benches and a pond. This is a suitable spot for a picnic or a rest but, as the sign on the gate suggests, do supervise children near the water.

Continue along the road with the church on your left. This road takes you out of the village and eventually towards open moorland, but first it veers right and passes over the trackbeds of two old railway lines that ran parallel with one another at this point. Looking right, and down the bank, you will see the former station, which has been lovingly maintained, complete with platform and signage even though it is now a private residence.

Station House, formerly Brentor Station (Author)

Brentor Station was built in 1890 from local granite. It was owned by the London & South Western Railway Company (later the Southern Region of British Railways) and was on the route that linked Waterloo with Plymouth. Closed as part of the Beeching reforms in the 1960s, the former station building is now family-owned and run as a Bed and Breakfast establishment. (There was no station here for the other line, which was once part of the Great Western Railway branch line from Plymouth to Launceston and closed in 1962.)

Pass over the cattle grid (or through the gate to one side) and follow the road straight ahead out onto the moorland. This road goes gently uphill, with Gibbet Hill rising away to the left. Follow the road until it reaches a sharp bend and then turn right into the road indicated as a 'no through road'. This road takes you over another cattle grid, passes Blacknor Park on the left and then becomes a gravelly track. As this track comes out of the trees, the remains of Wortha Mill will be seen on the right - just before a bridge.

Wortha Mill

According to information obtained locally, Wortha Mill dates back to around 200 years ago and up until the beginning of the 20th century was used for grinding corn. It was then used as a dwelling place for about 20 years, but has been uninhabited ever since.

Continue along the track as the bridge carries it over another part of the trackbeds of the two old railway lines, and also the River Burn, and then follow it uphill between the hedgerows, admiring the variety of fauna and flora they hold. At the next T-junction of tracks, turn left, go past South Brentor Farm (ignoring the road going off to the right) and continue to walk uphill. Follow this road for some distance, passing some delightful cottages with amazing views, until it bends sharply to the left. On the apex of the bend, go through the gate on the right and follow the indistinct track along the edge of the field, keeping the hedge to your left. You are now just below the Church of St. Michael of the Rock.

The Church of
St. Michael of the Rock (Author)

At the far end of the field, as you near the road once more, you will notice a fenced-off area on the right. Within this area are the remains of a 19th century manganese mine which was responsible for much employment in the local area between 1815 and 1856. The mineral obtained from here - used in the production of glass, bleach and steel - was transported via Morwellham Quay and the River Tamar.

Pass through the gate and join the road. Turn right - again taking great care to look out for traffic - and follow this road back to the car park.

Bibliography

Haunted Dartmoor, R. W. Bamberg (Peninsula Press, 1993)

Made in Devon, Chips Barber & David Fitzgerald (Obelisk Publications, 1988)

Ten Family Walks on Dartmoor, Sally & Chips Barber (Obelisk Publications, 2000)

Walking the Stories & Legends of Dartmoor, Michael Bennie (Peninsula Press, 1995)

St. Michael of the Rock with Christ Church, Charles K. Burton & Gerald L. Matthews (Tempest, 1990)

Crossing's Guide to Dartmoor, William Crossing (Peninsula Press,1990)

One Hundred Years on Dartmoor, William Crossing (Devon Books, 1987)

Stones of Dartmoor and their story, William Crossing (Quay Publications, 1987)

Unlock the History of Dartmoor Prison, (Dartmoor Prison Museum leaflet)

Walking in Southern Dartmoor, Dartmoor Rescue Group

High Dartmoor, Eric Hemery (Robert Hale, 1983)

St. Mary the Virgin, Holne, Holne Parochial Church Council (Bradford & Son, 1992)

A History of Holne, Villagers of Holne (1977)

The Water Babies, Charles Kingsley (Puffin, 1984)

Strange Stories from Devon, R. A. Lauder & M. Williams (Bossiney Books, 1982)

A Visitor's Guide to Dartmoor, John Pegg (John Pegg Publishing, 1984)

Dartmoor Inns, Tom Quick (Devon Books, 1992)

Holne, Dartmoor, Rev. W. H. Harvey Royse, RN (Church Print Co. 1920)

The Plymouth & Dartmoor Railway and The Lee Moor Tramway, Eric R. Shepherd (Ark Publications (Railways), 1997)

Walk Dartmoor, Peter Tavy (Bartholomew & Son, 1984)

Fifty Walks in Devon, Sue Viccars (AA Publishing, 2001)

Western Morning News, (21st April 1939, courtesy of Devon Library Services)